50 SHADES of Red

Her Story, His Love

GRACE CHAPEL

ARCHWAY
PUBLISHING

Archway Publishing books may be ordered through booksellers or by contacting:

Archway Publishing
1663 Liberty Drive
Bloomington, IN 47403
www.archwaypublishing.com
844-669-3957

ISBN: 978-1-6657-2320-6 (sc)
ISBN: 978-1-6657-2321-3 (e)

Library of Congress Control Number: 2022908320

Print information available on the last page.

Archway Publishing rev. date: 05/10/2022

This book is dedicated to God the Father,

God the Son, and God the Holy Spirit.

CONTENTS

FOREWORD

*W*ho better to write the foreword to this book than the author herself, in a third-person-omniscient viewpoint to provide readers with insight into multiple characters, the emotions of others, and meaningful thoughts? She was born and raised in *fifty* different palettes of corruption, including physical, spiritual, and sexual abuse topped with marital infidelity.

She features herself in good and bad relationships and explains the impact of sin from the womb to childhood to adulthood. She explains that hereditary, environment, and willfulness were the three angles through which transgression permeated her life. It took her more than fifty years to process and overcome her childhood traumas. So sit back and relax as we journey into her autobiography.

She entered this world like a champion. In the dark abyss of her mother's womb, she jetted out from the warmth of her father's flow and navigated to a mysterious incubator where she was formed in secrecy, carefully and meticulously assembled, nothing missing, every cell in its specific place.

Wow! What mastery. Perfect artistry by the mysterious hand of God.

Her physical features, spiritual virtue, and emotional intellect were all meshed together with divine purpose. In the secret place of her mother's womb, she was meticulously fashioned for greatness by the majestic hand of God (Ps. 139, NIV). He made her with an innate desire and longing to know, love, and worship Him. God essentially made her for God himself.

No doubt she was destined for good health, wealth, and greatness. The evils that happened after her birth will make you gasp for breath, clutch your pearls, and wonder if she was ever meant for anything good. Will she triumph over the evils that await her in a crouched-down position on her life's path? Well, stay focused, and we will find the answers together.

ACKNOWLEDGMENTS

I would like to acknowledge my two adult children, Sonday and Iva, who are the blessings of my womb. They were born in the right conditions of love and marriage. They are a direct result of a married couple in love with each other. I desired my children would be born in holy matrimony, and God gave me the desire of my heart. I love you, kiddos!

This book is also in memory of my grandmother, Elsie Whitehead, whose tireless prayers and love brought me to God.

INTRODUCTION

*G*od's rich mercies, goodness, and love brought this book to fruition. Premature death, imprisonment, a mental asylum, a loose and lascivious life, and that unquenchable blazing lake of fire called hell (Hades) were supposed to be her end result, but God ran interference and brought about the opposite. Every devil, person, place, and thing, had to bow down and obey the piercing presence of God in her life. He gave her eternal life, a perfectly sound mind, and a VIP seat in heavenly places with His darling Son Jesus Christ.

God made her a living witness to His restorative powers, a gifted and anointed preacher, an honorable military veteran, a mother of two fine adult children, a chaplain of prisoners, a restorer of the needy, and a woman endowed with the power of the Holy Spirit who fuels her to operate in five-fold ministries.

CHAPTER 1

What the Devil Planned

*C*rouching down at the foot of the delivery table, just waiting for the baby to come out of the birth canal, the devil began his attacks immediately. The doctor cut her umbilical cord too close to the stub on her tummy at birth. She was slated by Satan to die an early death, and several alternative death plots had been put into place:

- Three days after birth, she developed an omphalitis infection and was rushed back to the hospital. Doctors stopped the condition from spreading, and she was saved in the nick of time.

- At the ages of five and six, her childlike curiosity about the clouds caused her to tiptoe on high railings with a broomstick pointing toward the sky. She poked and stirred the air and what appeared to be the low-hanging clouds. Little did she know that one slip would have caused a sudden fall to her death.

- At the age of eight, she was almost killed by a motorcyclist speeding past the pedestrian walkway outside the elementary school gates. *Vroom, vroom, zoom!* She felt the swift breeze brush past her tender face. With her heart pounding out of her chest, she felt the scare and trembled at her brush with death.

- When she was twenty-one, a military-training exercise almost caused her death, but she was rescued and resuscitated.

- Five months pregnant with her second child, she was strapped into the passenger seat of the family car going home from a Mother's Day event when another car crashed into it from the back, causing a hard, swift jerk toward the windshield. After being rushed to the hospital by ambulance, baby and mother came out unharmed. The headline "Mother and Unborn Child Die in a Car Crash on

Mother's Day" never made the news. God's hedge of protection canceled every death plot of the devil.

- A domestic altercation occurred inside a fast-moving luxury car entering the highway at forty-five miles an hour. She snatched her seat belt in a frenzy to escape the physical attacks and swung the door wide open. She desperately threatened to jump out of the vehicle. "Let me out! Pull over! Let me out! Let me out or I'll jump! Stop the damn *car*!" Well, this road range came to an end. He stopped the car. She got out and stomped her way down the exit ramp, then went straight home. That pending news headline about a forty-nine-year-old woman jumping to her death from a fast-moving car on South Highway 95 never made it to the press because God canceled the fatality.

- Several other fights took place in cars. Swift jabs to the neck and rib cage were followed by a hot cup of coffee in the lap. The car made a U-turn and sped back to the house with screeching tires, pulled abruptly into the driveway, then slowly crawled into the garage. The car was parked with the windows rolled up. Boisterous prayers raised the roof of the car. Speaking with quivering tongues of fire, she continued tirelessly for ten minutes. Her actions put the most confused, insane look on his face. He stared at her and concluded in his mind, *She's got to be crazy.* Needless to say, that was the last car ride they took together, and the relationship was done. Kaput!

Since Satan's plans for premature death did not work, he chose to destroy her purity and innocence through rapes and molestations, so she would be stained for life and never reach the mark of holiness. As if she were slated for a life of pain, shame, and disgrace, wicked men positioned themselves in her path.

- One slid his hardness between her tender buttocks as she lay sleeping on the floor among her snoring siblings in a crowded one-bedroom hut. His favorite time to sleep-rape was in the darkness of night, when everyone else was sound asleep.

- Another wiggled and forced his masculine fingers straight up her vaginal walls. The friction of his rough fingers left her supple flesh bruised and bleeding. His favorite time to fondle and molest was at the Saturday midday matinee.

- A third one buggered her from the back every day after school in the second grade inside a church's presbytery.

- The fourth man lurked around the Promenade Gardens overlooking the children's playground. His twisted tactic was indecent exposure, which drew the child's attention to him. While her eyes were fixed in a stare, he rapidly jiggled his genitalia into combustion. His favorite time to perform was during playground recess.

- The rapist, molester, pedophile, and abusive uncle are all deceased. Nevertheless, they served as an initiation into the wickedness that would spoil her innocence and then transition her from victim to predator.

Warnings:

- Wicked people may die out, but the devilish spirits which possessed them, are still very much alive in the four corners of the earth; dwelling in both sacred and unsacred places. Predators may even move away from your geographical region but don't allow yourselves to be blindsided or gullible. Instead, be clearheaded and eagle-eyed because your enemy, the Devil, is tirelessly scouting after his next victim. Satan! Where have you come from? Satan answered God and said from going to and fro in the earth and walking up and down in it (Job2:2 ESV).

- Perverted spirits dwell in Family Circles, churches, schools, workplaces, prisons, jails, brothels, strip joints, drug rings, gang hangouts, rock bands, hip-hop groups, legal and illegal businesses, recording industries, human trafficking, just to mention a few, are targeted entities and sites for abusers and sex predators.

- Human beings are not necessarily the opponent of purity, but vessels through which impure spirits travel, transfer, and work. We do not wrestle against flesh and blood, but against powers, principalities, rulers of the darkness of this world, and spiritual wickedness in high places (Ephesians 6:12 KJV).

- Incubus, Succubus, spirit marriages and soul-ties are prevalent wherever mass numbers of people dwell. Married or unmarried, the objective is to possess a warm body through which they can carry out their sexually explicit and illicit practices against the weak and vulnerable, ultimately warring against God.

- A universal warning to all people is: Not everyone you see in a church, temple, tabernacle, synagogue, is demon possessed and in need of an exorcism. The opposite is also true, not everyone you see in a clergy position or title is completely delivered and committed to a life of holiness in God. The faith community is just like the melting pot of the world. It consists of a combination of good and evil, sheep and wolves, wheat and tares, and it is your responsibility to decipher the differences and remain devoted to the vision of Jesus Christ. He will return and skillfully separate and rapture those he reserved for himself.

- Awareness of wicked spirits, their objectives and vessels through which they work, are a good start to divine protection, Godly wisdom, counsel, and recovery.

CHAPTER 2

Deck Stacked

High

Quite frankly, this young girl had the deck stacked high against her—a deck of ungodly evils at the poker table of her life. As if she were molded as a pretty porcelain cup of pleasure for pedophiles, molesters, and rapists, they each drank their fill of her innocence. These evils occurred for five straight years, from the tender age of five all the way to ten.

A clergy card in the stack says, "Derailment of faith in God at any juncture in her life." Father Vincent was supposed to represent the love of God, but molesting innocent young girls in the back of the church's presbytery cast the wrong impression. God would no longer be seen as a loving person through the child's lens of experience.

A bastard baby card in the stack says, "Voluntary sexual

intercourse between the unmarried is to be a set pattern from birth and continued through adult life." The only thing that would break this bastard cycle would be direct interference from God himself. The bastard card also suggests a product molded for a life of ridicule, rejection, misunderstanding, sibling rivalry, and recurring episodes of family drama.

Outsiders and gossipers would have a field day nitpicking and picnicking over scraps of remarks void of supportive facts and evidence. Ouch! That's gotta hurt. Stained and stigmatized for life. When the bastard baby card is played, who walks away as the happy winner? Well, this is a very good question. Let's dig in to find the answer.

CHAPTER 3

Retaliation
Called Her

*C*hildhood traumas mixed with adult years of pain and regret were coupled on a loud bullhorn, calling at her to come and quell this desire to retaliate and avenge through strings of vigilante activities.

At first, she was a little child, frail and defenseless, with no thoughts of harming anyone ever. But the tables turned, and she became an adult with military training, defensive tactics, war strategies, and a boldness to serve and protect, fight of the hardest of criminals, overthrow the bad guys, accomplish the mission, and return home. She could have easily gone after her predators and justified her premeditated actions. Drown 'em in the pool. Shove 'em down the stairs. Smother 'em with a pillow. The LORD kept her from bloodshed and from avenging herself with her own hands, as he did in the story of David and Nabal (1Samuel 25:26 ESV).

An awakening came to her through a small still voice within. What are you going to do with the word of life that is hidden in your heart? What are you going to do with the rivers of living waters inside your belly? Do they not work together to comfort the innocent, convict the guilty, and bring them to justice? Wasn't the Word and Spirit of God sent to victims and predators alike?

Therefore, if you answer the call to retaliation, you must also answer the call to imprisonment, because they go together. Retaliate, and you get government-issued prison garb, a prison-felon ID card, an assigned prison cell, and a colored armband signifying the classification of your crime and the length of your stay in prison.

What if she opened her eyes and saw herself in ranks with those inmates she served as chaplain once upon a time? Wouldn't it be the epitome of hypocrisy, shame, and disgrace? Yes, you are exactly right. This is the awakening she came to.

If you have ever been hurt to this extreme, you have every right to feel angry and bitter, and to have a deep, gnawing desire to take revenge. I thought, *Blast them all away one after the other, execution-style, then walk away from the scene like they never existed.* For a brief moment, such a reaction might bring satisfaction. But the consequences of inner guilt, shame, and blood-stained hands for life say, "Think about it long and hard, then reconsider." Yes, we suffer at the hands of evil, heinous men, but none of them is worth spending our lives in prison and going to that eternal lake of fire.

The Bible says vengeance belongs to the Lord. He will repay when we leave it all to Him (Heb. 10:30, ESV). Taking matters into my own hands would be a blatant disregard for this passage of scripture. I would bring indictment on my soul for knowing God's Word and still violate its precepts. Anyone who lives by the sword dies by the sword (Matt. 26:52, ASV). Forgive seventy times seven (Matt. 18:21–22, KJV). These truths are glaring maps that, when applied properly, serve as roadblocks to potentially self-destructive behaviors.

It is so good to know scriptures that apply to your specific situation, but it's even better to actively do what they say. You don't have to do God's part; you only have to let the Word heal you and be fully restored to the life of wholeness

God intended for you. Innocent people die when they get caught in the crossfire of a gang shooting. Bullets intended for the opposing gangsters hit and kill innocent bystanders.

So it is when we get caught in the crossfire of a war between God and Satan. In the wrong place at the wrong time when two opposing forces aim their ammunitions at each other; but because we positioned ourselves in the middle of the crosshairs we suffer accidental injuries and/or death. The only rule of thumb victims have to remember is you will not have to fight this battle. Take up your positions stand firm and see the deliverance the Lord will give you (2 Chronicles 20:17 ESV). When you feel afraid that you will die at the hands of your enemy just remember, the Lord will fight for you and all you have to do is hold your peace (Exodus 14:14 ESV).

CHAPTER 4

Forgiveness

J esus Christ was tempted in the desert by the devil, but He answered with the written Word of God. I have been forgiven of my past, present, and future sins. Therefore, I must now forgive my offenders of the past, present, and future offenses committed against me. If those whom God has forgiven do not release forgiveness to others, they have ticketed themselves a first-class shuttle to hell. Jesus did not stutter when He said, "But if you do not forgive others their sins, your Father will not forgive your sins" (Matt. 6:15, NIV).

There are many ways to start your journey of forgiveness:

- Release forgiveness to all who have harmed you. Say it verbally and write it down.

- Begin to distribute those 70 x 7 (490) forgiveness cards.

- If your perpetrators are deceased, write their names on the backs of the cards and release them into a river or a bonfire, or place the cards on the altar at church and walk away.

- Remember God as a type of bounty hunter who chases after the bad guys, catches up with them, and brings them to justice.

- If you need a mental-health professional to help you process your past, do it with confidence, knowing your end is full restoration and a peaceful life.

- Find a Holy Ghost–anointed church and jump into the praise and worship. Let the joy of the Lord be your strength. In His presence, there's fullness of joy, and at His right hand, pleasures forevermore. God will trade your mourning for dancing, and your grieving for praise (Ps. 30:11–12, Ps. 16:11, Neh. 8:10, Hab. 3:18, NKJ).

- Go ahead and cry out loud, shout for joy, and praise the Lord, like you're the only one in the building. Pray out loud. Vent your grievance to God. Write a song about Him and sing it out loud. These are far better coping mechanisms than drugs, sex, and cold-blooded crimes. The blood of Jesus

Christ is adequate enough to cover all of your sins past present and future. To keep himself from remembering your offenses he tossed him into the sea forgetfulness as far as the east is from the west. His blood is also adequate enough to cover all the sins of your predators the same way. If by chance, your offenders came to know him in the pardoning of their sins, God has also tossed their offenses in the sea of forgetfulness as far as the east is from the west. Remember, no one has the authority to undo the finished work of Jesus Christ.

Her Love Note To Him

To the God I love with all my heart, soul, mind, and strength: All honor and the highest praises to God my Father, Jesus my Lord, and my seal, the Holy Spirit in my life. Thank you for the salvation of my soul, the baptism of the Holy Ghost, and the peace like a river that floods my soul. In my fifty-five years of life, I have discovered for myself that there is no distance (height, width, length, depth, circumference, or perimeter) too far for the God of all flesh to reach me. God, your presence transcends and permeates every single barrier. You have proven to me that there is no darkness you cannot brighten, no stain too ingrained to remove. You are my personal Lord and personal savior who saved me from the depths of hell, Satan's powers, and my own self-willed offenses.

You are the steady ray of light in the midst of my dark moments, my scouring agent who removed the bloody stains of past guilt and shame. You sent me deliverers who rescued me from the hands of my enemies and redirected my footsteps, unseen angels who kept me from suffocating at the hands of my molesters, a grandmother of faith who modeled the gospel, a military colleague who introduced life in reading the Bible, warnings through visions and dreams, and revelations by the Holy Ghost.

Your divine interventions at different intervals prevented me from committing crimes of vengeance against my perpetrators. Hallelujah to the God and lover of my soul! Forever be lifted and glorified in my life. Your fingerprints are on every page of my story. No doubt You are truly the author and finisher of my faith. For these things, I will always love and praise you. I laud and magnify your name. I join in with the company of Heaven saying "'Holy, holy, holy is the Lord God Almighty,' who was, and is, and is to come" (Rev. 4:8, NIV).

His Love Note To Her:

Dear Grace,

You are my beautiful treasure. You are the apple of my eyes and I positioned you on the high hanging branches of the tree of life, so that no devouring foe can pluck you from my reach. Not only are you pleasant to my eyes, but you are also on my mind day and night. I think about you so many times in one day it out numbers the grains of sand on the sea shores. Whenever I think about you it is always good and nothing evil. I gear my thoughts towards a hope and a future for you.

I cannot bear a single thought of leaving you. So I made a vow, never to leave nor forsake you. My love for you is not temporal like the love of earthly men. My love is everlasting, even after death you will open your eyes and see me face to face again. Your Physical spiritual and emotional flaws, are nothing but beauty marks to me. I voluntarily died on your behalf. From the time I laid eyes on you, I knew I would be the one for you and you for me. I am my beloved and my beloved is mine.

It is my good pleasure to be your husbandman, who looks beyond your faults and sees all your desperate needs for me. Love will always be the banner I hang over you. With an unfailing love I have drawn you to myself. I exhort jealous care over you. I say to everyone back up! hands off! She is not for sale. Grace, you are all mine. Until we meet again in the secrecy of your prayer closet, remember I am forever, the lover of your soul.

CHAPTER 5

Eyewitness

*I*f I didn't know better, I would say I've seen it all. I have witnessed the vices that intrude on and destroy good relationships. Sitting in the front-row seat of the theater of life, I had a close-up view of several relationships that included adultery, infidelity, fornication, incest, crossbreeding, stepchildren, and the consequences of separation and divorce. Quite frankly, I've had more than what I'm willing to share in this book.

The dynamics of each relationship were way too complex to comb through every single gory detail. So I have opted for the bony framework of a bulleted outline. I had a close-up view of several relationships:

- In the first, two adults (one man, one woman), married to their own spouses, fell for each other despite their marital status. These two cheaters conceived a baby together and kept it a secret from their spouses. Later on, the child grew up and discovered that the man she called Daddy was actually her stepfather. Oh, what a mess to clean up!

Were you a product of adultery? The Bible teaches that every man should have his own wife and every woman her own husband. Whatsoever state you're in, learn to be content. The secret of being content, godliness with contentment, is great gain. If you are unmarried, be single and satisfied.

If you are married, be committed and content with the one you have. If you lied your way to the top, come back down to honesty and integrity, and these vices will not be hereditarily passed down to the next generation.

The married man went home and made love to his wife and made her pregnant. By the time the baby was born, he had fathered another child outside his marriage. The woman with whom he fathered the child had a husband of her own plus three children belonging to other men. A good takeaway lesson from this is don't have sex with another person's spouse. Read chapter 7 in this book, and learn what the Bible has to say about adultery and cooperate with its principles. Those who do not acknowledge their sin and repent for it cannot spend eternity in Heaven and will be locked outside the gates. Any person who covers his or her sins shall not prosper.

As time went on, the two couples' children intermingled with each other, and as a result, inappropriate incestuous relationships developed. At one point, they all attended the same school, where other students questioned the authenticity of their relationships. Were they true relatives or just boyfriend/girlfriend drawn to each other? It will be well worth your time to explore sibling relations according to the Bible.

- I witnessed another scene in which a young man went into his stepsister, then into his adopted sister, and later on, a stepfather slept with the stepdaughter. These were the epitome of inappropriate relations. A good takeaway lesson from this scene is sex with siblings is a carnal sin. Read chapter 7 for the pertaining Bible verse. Teach yourself what the Bible has to say about overstepping family boundaries in kinship relationships.

- In one scene, I saw this young girl coming out the doorway of my father's bedroom in the wee hours of the morning. I may have only been a little girl back then, but I knew that the purpose of a bedroom is for sleeping in the bed. Something was definitely off with this picture. I smelled a fish, and there was no aquarium in the house.

A good takeaway lesson from this scene is that little pictures have big ears, so be careful what you do in front of them, because they also have eyes. My grandmother Elsie always said little pictures are symbolic of little children. Be careful what you say and do in front of them. They are likely to remember it forever. I adopted this concept and began to live as if I were on *Candid Camera* every day. This way, I'm mindful of my actions, and strive to be squeaky clean, never caught doing anything I do not want public eyes to see.

- A divorced man took an interest in a divorced woman. He proposed to give her happiness all the days of her life. She accepted his offer and married him. Just one year into the marriage, she found out his definition of happiness was erotic sex. Without it, his night was spoiled, and his mornings were miserable. They quarreled every day, back and forth, about his sex addiction until the marriage ended with an explosion: A long strand of brunette hair on the passenger's side of the car, followed by a mailed package of homosexual artifacts from a gay man in Texas.

   A good takeaway lesson from this episode is to find out the definition of happiness before you marry someone. For some, it's money; for others, it's sex. In other cases, it might be unconditional love and a strong faith-based life. Know the differences before committing yourself to marriage, especially a second or third time around.

- A single man took an interest in a single woman. They had a happy marriage with two beautiful children.

Over two decades later, an old acquaintance from the past stole his heart and ended his marriage.

A good takeaway lesson from this one is to clean out the search history, cache, phone contacts, questionable selfies, and questionable photographs with personal friends from all social networks and even consider a brand-new phone and telephone number before going into marriage. Once you are married, these old acquaintances can show up and break up a marriage you thought would last forever.

- A rich old couple found a young woman fit to marry their Son. They wanted to have grand children of their own, expand the family lineage, maintain the family wealth, and keep the family business running. They made great lavish arrangements and organized everything necessary for the wedding. They did everything behind her back and kept the young woman in the dark. After a while, their secret got out, and the young girl escaped to safety. The old rich couple hung their heads in guilt and shame. They were foolish, manipulative, and deceitful in trying to trick an innocent young girl into marriage.

A few good takeaway points are: Never arrange a marriage in the land of the free in the 21st century. This is the custom in middle eastern civilization not necessarily in the west. A totalitarian mindset exercises an extremely high degree of control in regulation over public and private life. These are those that are not American minded nor Christian minded as they may seem.

The Christian viewpoint says: If you desire a friend show yourself friendly, be hospitable to strangers, do good to all people, especially the saints, be in sacred fellowship with each other, develop a good rapport, let your speech be seasoned with grace not judgment, and dwell with others according to the knowledge drawn from sincere friendship. Exercise holy restraints until marriage. Greet each other with a holy kiss, just as scripture says.

Keeping these truths in mind, it is better to marry on the basis of real heartfelt, genuine love; not as a result of a forced, arranged, matchmaking parents, nor controlling mandates. If parents force their way into their children's marriage, how much real privacy will the married couple really have in the long run? Will they also dibble and dabble in the couples sex life to hasten the making of grand children? Of course they will. Their actions at the door describes who they are. Controlling matchmakers will stick around to make sure everything goes their way. A forced, sham, and fake marriage is only for convenience and selfish ambitions. The core of it all is master manipulation, deception and witchcraft; not a holy matrimony at all.

Evil seeds of corruption planted in the beginning or foundation of a marriage will sprout up, and blossom into more corrupt fruit in the longevity of the marriage; unless God runs interference, tills the soil, breaks up the fallow grounds, and brings a change.

In America, marriage fraud is a felony punishable by five years in prison and $250,000 fine. Today I thank God for being my refuge and my strength, a very present help in time of trouble. I was indeed a close-up eyewitness to more wickedness than I wish to disclose.

CHAPTER 6

Running Interference

*T*he vices of double adultery, double fornication, intermixed relations, incest, deception, manipulations, lustful venues, and their potentially destructive influence created such a sin crisis that *only a miracle work of God* could fix it.

God intervened and rescued me from disgrace and sin. He reserved me for Himself and future glory. He would run interference by sending Christian-hearted people in various dimensions to plant seeds of godliness in my life.

Grandma Elsie was one of them. She saw to it that I drank the holy water—a page from the Bible containing the 23rd Psalm rolled up like a scroll and placed in a small bottle with water. "Come now!" she said. "Drink up, it's good for you!"

I trusted my granny more than I trusted anyone else in

the whole world. Her maternal instincts could detect problems and solutions in one shot. Sometimes the smallest insignificant action is the solution to a big problem. I didn't know it then, but I sure know it now. Holy water is a sacred element that wards off evil spirits and evil influences.

In scripture, it was spit mixed with mud that Jesus rubbed on a blind man's eyes. That didn't make sense either, but it sure did work. The blind man declared, "First I was blind, but now I can see" (John 9:25 KJV).

If your grandmother was anything like mine, there was never a shortage of homemade recipes in the kitchen, nor homemade remedies for any ailment in the family. Sometimes the beginning and the middle of a situation do not make sense, but the end results explain everything. My granny knew my vulnerability and need for protection from evil spirits.

Between herself and God inside her little prayer closet, I needed highly anointed supernatural protection from God. Looking back, I can tell the spirit, wisdom, and counsel of God were with my grandmother. In her daily devotion to God, she positioned herself on the floor at the foot of her bed with an open Bible in her hands. Silent quivering prayers flowed from her lips. Any given day, a glimpse of the small-framed old lady with thick bifocal reading glasses on her face could be seen, whispering sounds coming from her lips. She was never in a rush or a hurry to get to the finish.

Her daily routine was a type of Christian road map directing my life for years to come. Each encounter with a Christian-hearted person like Granny Elsie drew my attention closer and closer toward a personal relationship with Jesus Christ.

Later on, in chapter 15, you'll read about how the baptism of the Holy Ghost was the cleansing agent God used to power-wash me of environmental, hereditary, and self-willed sins. As a result, my life began to take a turn for the good. Permit the interference of God in your life, because the end result is a better you, blessings beyond measure, an escape from life in prison which is the penance of government, and an escape from eternal damnation, which is reserved for the devil and the disobedient (Rev. 22:15 KJV).

Takeaways

- Permit the interference of God in your life. He often uses relatives, friends, and even strangers to get you back on track. The least we can do is be on the lookout for those who God has poured himself into because He gave them something to pour into you.

- Receive those He sends across your path. They are equipped with the nuggets you need to survive your past and press toward the mark of the high calling in Christ Jesus (Phil. 3:13–14 KJV). People who nudge you toward the things of God bear the spirit of the fear of the Lord. The remaining six are the Spirit of the Lord, wisdom, understanding, counsel, might, and knowledge—a company to transition from victim to a victorious lifestyle (Rev. 5:6 KJV).

- Pass on the spirit of God to the next generation. Your study of the seven spirits of God is well worth your time. You take on their traits, and they live through you.

    The spirits of God are healing virtues. Peter passed the Holy Spirit of God to a lame man when he said, "Silver or gold I do not have, but what I do have I give you. In the name of Jesus Christ of Nazareth, walk." (Acts 3:6, NIV) Needless to say, the man got up, leapt for joy, and walked in praise of God.

CHAPTER 7

Discovering Truth

J ust when I thought this is the way life is supposed to be—full of hurt, pain, abuse, deception, and manipulation—a new chapter came open when I began to discover biblical truths. Through reading the Bible, my eyes became open to things that are right versus wrong, ethical versus unethical, moral versus immoral, wise versus foolish, the righteous versus the wicked, and sins versus virtues, just to mention a few.

A brand new world of knowledge, a brand new perspective of life, and an evolving new person began to form. There were cultural traditions, generational practices, and self-sabotaging behaviors that had to be cut off of my life completely.

When I was twenty-one, I met a Christian young man in the military who presented me with a challenge to read the Bible. I gave my life to Jesus Christ and got baptized before I left for military service. But after salvation, there is a need for spiritual growth and development, and this is what God did to ensure I had a deeper, closer relationship with Him.

This young man was a key instrument in a proper spiritual transition for my life. Although he spoke the English language, his conversation sounded foreign because he pointedly spoke about God and the Bible. His conduct was pious, saintly, and restrained, which was quite the opposite of what I knew men to be. The young man's behaviors were void of overtures, fraternization, flirting, and the common hissing of men.

One day, he posed a challenge question: "How do you know how to live if you do not read the Bible?" I accepted the Bible challenge. As soon as I began to read the Bible, my eyes, ears, and heart swung wide open to compare and contrast God's ways with my own—programmed from childhood, most modeled by parents and siblings, a few of my own self-made.

While reading the Holy Bible, I quickly realized a contradiction between its guidelines and my standards. I began to learn and absorb what the Bible says about unlawful sexual relations. I discovered the following truths in the book of Leviticus:

The Lord said to Moses, "Speak to the Israelites and say to them I am the Lord your God. You *must not do as they do* in Egypt, where you used to live, and you must *not do as they do* in the land of Canaan where I am bringing you. *Do not follow* their practices. You must obey my laws and be careful to follow my decrees. I am the Lord your God. Keep my decrees and laws, for the person who abases them will live by them. I am the Lord.

"**No one** is to approach any close relative to have sexual relations. I am the Lord.

"**Do not** dishonor your father by having sexual relations with your mother. She is your mother; **do not** have relations with her.

"**Do not** have sexual relations with your father's wife; that would dishonor your father.

"**Do not** have sexual relations with your sister, either your father's daughter or your mother's daughter, whether she was born in the same home or elsewhere.

"'**Do not** have sexual relations with your son's daughter or your daughter's daughter; that would dishonor you.

"'**Do not** have sexual relations with the daughter of your father's wife born to your father; she is your sister.

"'**Do not** have sexual relations with your father's sister; she is your father's close relative.

"'**Do not** have sexual relations with your mother's sister, because she is your mother's close relative.

"'**Do not** dishonor your father's brother by approaching his wife to have sexual relations; she is your aunt.

"'**Do not** have sexual relations with your daughter-in-law. She is your son's wife; do not have relations with her.

"'**Do not** have sexual relations with your brother's wife; that would dishonor your brother.

"'**Do not** have sexual relations with both a woman and her daughter. **Do not** have sexual relations with either her son's daughter or her daughter's daughter; they are her close relatives. That is wickedness

"'**Do not** take your wife's sister as a rival wife and have sexual relations with her while your wife is living.

"'**Do not** approach a woman to have sexual relations during the uncleanness of her monthly period.

"'**Do not** have sexual relations with your neighbor's wife and defile yourself with her.

"'**Do not** give any of your children to be sacrificed to Molek, for **you must not profane** the name of your God. I am the Lord.

"'**Do not** have sexual relations with a man as one does with a woman; that is detestable.

"'**Do not** have sexual relations with an animal and defile yourself with it. A woman must not present herself to an animal to have sexual relations with it; that is a perversion.

"**Do not** defile yourselves in any of these ways, because this is how the nation that I am going to drive out before you became defiled. Even the land was defiled; so I punished it for its sin, and the land vomited out its inhabitants. But you must keep my decrees and my laws. The native-born and the foreigners residing among you **must not do any of these detestable things**, for all these things were done by the people who lived in the land before you, and the land became defiled. And if you defile the land, it will vomit you out as it vomited out the nations that were before you.

"'Everyone who does any of these detestable things—such persons must be cut off from their people. Keep my requirements and **do not** follow any of the detestable customs that were practiced before you came and do not defile yourselves with them. I am the Lord your God. (Leviticus 18, NIV).

I began to understand what sin is, how God feels about

it, and the various penalties and consequences. For instance, since Ruben went into his father's concubine on the couch, his Father Jacob pronounced him a curse not to excel in life (Gen. 35:22, Gen. 49:1–4, NIV). Since neither Adam nor Eve obeyed God's instructions in the Garden of Eden, they were expelled from it (Gen. 3:23–24, ISV). By these two examples sin always brings consequences.

It is well worth your time to learn the boundaries of godly sexuality in Leviticus 18:6–29. These truths from God's word save one from a perpetual cycle of generational vices and behaviors viewed as natural and/or normal because everyone around you does them.

My eyes have been opened to sin and its definition (which is an immoral word, thought, and act against God's law). It would be well worth your time to look up the following nine stories and characters in the Bible. The nine examples are not a license to mimic immoral behavior but avoid the entrapment of them.

1. Amnon and Tamar- a brother raped his own sister
2. Judah and Tamar- a father-in-law impregnated his daughter-in-law with twins

3. Gomar and Hosea- a prophet married a whore

4. Three sins of Rachel- stole her sister's husband, nephew's aphrodisiac, and prattled

5. God killed Onan- spilled semen

6. Twins Oholah and Oholibah- failed to learn from each other's mistakes

7. Ham against his father, Noah- children violated their own parents

8. Jezebel, killer and prostitute- devoured by dogs

9. Ahitophel and Absalom -sex on the roof top, was ungodly advise

Sharpen your awareness. Fight for a life of purity. Expand your knowledge of what the Bible has to say about purity versus sexual immorality. Do your part to stop the senseless pain, destruction, and death that comes from a lack of knowledge. Of course, don't limit yourself to these nine stories; there are many more like them to learn from in the Bible.

CHAPTER 8

Uncle/Father

I took a trip down memory lane and remembered my first taste of trickery and deception. A nice-smelling man in clean clothes, with gold jewelry around his neck and fingers, visited the house regularly, especially on Friday and Saturday nights. He swooped me up and off to the burger palace to eat and play. I had so much fun slurping a thick strawberry milkshake and hot cheeseburger with pickles. Afterward, I hopped back into the blue Dodge Avenger pickup truck.

The man's name was Mr. Vernon, but I was made to call him Uncle Vernon, affectionately. In those days. It was family custom and cultural mannerism that every female visitor is called auntie and every male visitor is called uncle out of respect for elders.

However, by age twelve, I had become a young lady in puberty. A phone call came through, and it was Uncle Vernon with a question: "Is there something you'd like to tell me?"

No! Oh yeah, I got my period today. Oh, but wait a minute, I thought, *wait just a minute, isn't this a personal matter, and why must I tell Uncle Vernon about it?* Well, that's a good question. Perhaps a higher power was beaming rays of light on kinship truth.

Hand-me-downs were a common practice for large families. When the eldest child grew out of clothes and shoes, the next child in line got to wear them until they no longer ft. My shoes were tight on my feet, and I needed a new pair for school. My feet were always the biggest among my siblings; none of their shoes could fit me either.

Suddenly, I was instructed to walk to my father's house to get money to buy a pair of shoes. *Wait ... what? Walk? To my father's house? I have another father? Oh, I see! I get it.* That pleasant-smelling man called Uncle Vernon was actually my biological father. In my first twelve years of life, I was calling my stepfather "Daddy" and my father "Uncle Vernon."

Seeds of Deception.

Like a hard slap in the face, that news ricocheted my brain. Confusion, deception, and shame flooded the space between my ears. What appeared to be a nice man treating a bunch of children with snacks, outings, and trips was actually a man with a guilty conscience doing his child-support visitations.

It was just like a glass of ice-cold water splashed in my face from across the table. I was a stepchild. Those with whom I grew up were stepsisters and stepbrothers. At age twelve, deep emotions of manipulation, deception, low self-esteem, deprivation, and a slew of other feelings surfaced from time to time throughout the years.

That day at the shoe store, I expected Uncle Vernon to do his usual: dip into his pocket, open his thick wallet stuffed with cash, and pay for my shoes, in the same way he'd paid for those outings he took me on. Instead, he popped a surprising question that left my twelve-year-old jaw on the floor: "Don't you have money to buy your own shoes?"

Until then, no one had ever asked me to pay for anything in my entire twelve years of living. At age twelve, who was I supposed to get money from to buy shoes for my steadily growing feet? I don't quite know when I did it, but a strong determination to have my own things, find a job, and be self-sufficient began to take shape. Having to walk miles away to my newly discovered father's house was another heavy responsibility on this young girl's mind.

Two Home-Wreckers

! Greedy! *Double greed* barely describes a married man with children who takes a woman belonging to someone else. *Greedy* is a married woman with children who takes a man belonging to someone else. They both have insatiable sexual appetites, which one person alone cannot fulfill. They're like drug addicts and alcoholics, who are known to benefit from AA and NA rehabilitative support. However, sex addicts deny, blame, and excuse the problem as ordinary acts of humanness.

"I'm only human" is a common excuse used by those who continue in the insatiable lust of the flesh. No consideration is given to how one's illicit behaviors affect innocent children. These innocents are left to face a life of perpetual hostility, conflict, sickness, destruction, broken relationships, broken hearts, and broken lives.

Harming the Least

Such evils invoke the wrath of God because children are dear to His heart. All babies are a heritage from Heaven (Ps. 127:3, NIV). They are innocent and defenseless, yet they suffer the consequences of adults' and their parents' transgressions. The defenseless child caught in the crossfire of this madness has a promise from God: total retaliation for one who brings harm to a child—a millstone tied around the neck and drowned in the middle of the sea (Matt. 18:6, NIV).

CHAPTER 9

Reacting to Adultery

*T*he typical knee-jerk reaction of a woman whose husband gets caught in adultery is nothing short of a saint turned into a raging-mad fire-spitting dragon, until everything and everyone who caused her pain is either dead or dying. The man who took her hand in marriage promised to love her and cherish her until death would them part, but he was unfaithful and fathered a child.

A wife and a mistress got pregnant in the same year by the same man. You can bet your last dollar: no woman on earth would refuse the opportunity to retaliate in some way, form, or fashion. Whether she is heard talking about it to others or silently thinks about it, revenge becomes the only itch she needs to scratch.

Tires are slashed, windows are bashed in, clothes and furniture are set on fire, testicles are cut and castrated. Then his whore shows up as a corpse on the side of the road. This is just a snippet of what she can do if the opportunity presents itself.

Judah and Tamar

There is a Judah in every man and a Tamar in every woman. Judah makes promises haphazardly, which he knows he does not intend to fulfill. Tamar prepares and positions herself to take her portion in life. She is a skilled actress by nature, born to perform on the stage of life, bringing nothing but Oscar-winning attention to herself. She played the role of a prostitute in Scripture to obtain the baby that would be promised through marriage to Judah's youngest son.

It is well worth your time to learn the consequences of broken promises, unfaithfulness, and hypocrisy taught us in Judah's intimacy with his daughter-in-law (Gen. 38 NIV). He thought he was sleeping with a hooker. He didn't know it was his daughter-in-law in disguise.

Truths from God's word can keep us from falling. A

woman has the potential to do whatever it takes to get what is rightfully hers.

A Typical Husband's Reaction to Adultery

What man would forgo the chance to strangle the Don Juan who gyrated on his wife and made her pregnant? Would he not be overcome with anger, malice, and revenge? It is pretty understandable, whether it was just a knee-jerk reaction or a contemplated reaction. *Just bust a cap in his nut sack; he ain't gonna hump another woman again. Nope, not on my watch!*

A man who lies with a married man's wife is a complete fool. He brings about his own destruction. He will suffer disease and disgrace and never be free from shame. The woman's husband will be jealous and angry and do everything he can to get revenge. No payment, no amount of money will stop him (Prov. 6:29–35, NIV).

CHAPTER 10

Sin Crisis

I know the commands of God, but I noticed another direction at work within my members. The law of sin wrestles with the law of God. As suggested in Romans 7:15-20 (NIV), when I set out to do the right thing, I end up doing that which is wrong; therefore, the things I really should do I do not do. Evil is everywhere I go. What I want to do, I do not do, but what I hate, I do. If I do what I do not want to do, I agree that the law is good. It is no longer by myself who does it but sin living in me. I know that nothing good lives in me that is in my sinful nature.

Because of these Bible-based truths, our hearts are not always in harmony with God's word. This is why we are in a sin crisis. Our bombarding self-destructive thoughts must be arrested, pulled down, and beat down into tiny dust particles, ready to be blown away like chaff in a gale. Tear them down aggressively until they resemble the written word: "Whatever is true, whatever is noble, whatever is right, whatever is pure, whatever is lovely, whatever is admirable—if anything is excellent or praiseworthy—think about such things." (Phil. 4:8, NIV)

Consider the following:

- It is noble to police the human mind properly with the word of God. Like every good police officer knows the rules by the book, we must have a working knowledge of God's law to put ourselves in check.

- Science teaches that the average human being has more than six thousand thoughts per day. If we tried to track the number of silent sins committed by the brain alone per day, it would shock us into a stupor. We would discover that we have underestimated our sins. The number is far greater than we think. To put matters in a nutshell, God said, "Your ways and thoughts are not mine; as far as Heaven is from the earth, so are my ways and thoughts *higher* than yours" (paraphrased from Isa. 55:8–9, NIV).

- The human mind and habits must be changed, renewed, and synchronized with God the Father's holiness (Phil. 2:5, Rom. 12:2, Phil. 4:8, NIV). These things are instrumental to God's command: "Be thou Holy as your heavenly Father is also Holy."

- We are a fallen, broken, estranged people whose sins God can smell (Rev. 18:5–15, Isa. 65:5, NIV).

- No exceptions: we have *all* succumbed to Satan's seduction since birth (Ps. 51:5, Rom. 3:23-24, NIV).

- If we say we have no sin, we are deniers of the truth, living in spiritual denial (1 John 1:8, Rom. 1:25, NIV).

- The penalty for sin/unholiness is destruction, death, and eternal damnation (Rom. 6:23, NIV).

A Prayer Guide for the Sin Crisis

Lord, I adore your name. I confess every ounce of my unworthiness. I have sinned against you with my words, thoughts, and deeds. I thank you for a straight and narrow path out of my sin crisis. I pray that you forgive me, save, heal, and deliver me from all hereditary, environmental, and self-willed sins.

Wash me in Your Blood, in fuller's soap, with hyssop,

and purify me in your refiner's fire. Fill me anew with your Holy Ghost. I pray that you hold me steadfastly in your care. Grace me to love, honor, and obey you with all of my heart, mind, and soul; not just today, but for all the days of my life. In Jesus's name, I pray. Amen!

CHAPTER 11

One Answer

The Sufficiency of Christ Jesus

F or the number of offenses you committed against others, Jesus Christ is a full sufficient payment for your sins. The number of sins other people have committed against you—Jesus Christ's blood is still a complete and adequate sacrifice for *their* sins. Bear in mind, sin requires bloodshed for proper redemption. If this were not so, Jesus Christ would not have said to the Apostle Paul, *My grace is sufficient for thee.* To the thief hanging on the cross, *"This day you will be with me in paradise.* To the tax collector Zacchaeus, *This day salvation has come to your house.* These, my friends, are a few examples for the epitome of grace.

Before Jesus came to earth, prophets, priests, kings, and animal sacrifices were not enough to solve the world's sin problem. Jesus came because only God's divine blood running through Jesus Christ's veins was sufficient to save all sinners. It was complete, final, perfect, and sufficient for the whole world (Heb. 10:1–18, Matt. 1:23, NIV). We must now intentionally choose to return to the one who paid the highest blood price for our souls.

Sin left us jacked up—torn up from the floor up. The holy image and likeness of God in humankind (Gen. 1:26, NIV) has been marred, scarred, hijacked, and slated by the devil for eternal damnation, to spend all of eternity in the lake of fire. Thank God for the shed blood of Jesus Christ, which brought salvation to the world. Acceptance of this truth begins the makeover process and reconciliation back to God.

Ministry of the Holy Spirit

Accepting the finished work of Jesus Christ saves the soul from eternal damnation, Satan's grasp, and individual self-willed sins. Accepting the ministry of the Holy Spirit empowers us to live a sin-free life following the commandments of God. It is true that if we walk in the Spirit, we will not fulfill the lust of the flesh (Gal. 5:16, NIV).

If the lust of the flesh is not fulfilled, then the will of God is engaged in divine glory. Practice His presence, listen to

His still voice, meditate on His word, show obedience to His will, and allow the soul to crave, hunger, and thirst for more of His presence. Through this Holy Spirit of God, sweetness is experienced outside of the bondage of sin and destruction.

When we sin as a result of living in a fallen world, we have an advocate with the Father, Jesus Christ, the righteous one (1 John 2:1, NIV), elder brother and high priest (Mark 3:34–35, Heb. 3:1, NIV). When sin leaves us spellbound and dumbfounded, the Holy Ghost of God is our intercessor, who intercedes on our behalf in prayer. He can eradicate those bombarding six thousand thoughts per day and seven thousand words per day, plus bring to the surface all truth learned from the word of God. He empowers us with spiritual fire and passion within—to live holy, righteous, pleasing, and acceptable lives unto God.

His Finished Works

As mentioned above in the first paragraph in the first chapter; Jesus Christ offered up a complete and perfect sacrifice for the sins of the world. Salvation comes only by believing this simple word of truth. Nothing else needs to be added to the finished works of Jesus Christ. He himself said *it is finished* while hanging from the cross. The fathers will and plan for saving the world through his Son Jesus is completed. He is only returning for those who believe He is all that scripture says he is.

An anonymous letter written to God reads: Dear God my records show they are many souls who snuck into heaven without a work-slip. Please line them up and send the following list of people back to earth; the thief on the cross, Mephibosheth the dead dog-man, Rahab the prostitute, Mary the demon possessed, David the murderer & adulterer, that woman caught in adultery, Paul the wretched man and persecutor of Christians, Isaiah the prophet with unclean lips, and that Moses guy the murderer.

God replied: *Dear writer, if work-slips could save souls, I would not have sent my Son to face the cross. I would've told him to stay put because smart people on earth have this all figured out. Stock piles of work-slips for the salvation of souls. Ha ha ha! You're a day late and a dollar short, or should I say 2000 years late and 2000 dollars short. My begotten Son already paid the full and highest price on Golgotha's hill.*

Works proceeds faith, therefore one must work out his

souls salvation. Each will be judged according to his deeds. Works accompanies faith, and faith by itself is dead. By grace one is saved, not by works, otherwise mere mortals will boast forever. All good works are as filthy rags. What is the value of filthy rags to the most Holy and High God? Absolutely none. My free gift to all the souls in the world is eternal life, through the finished works of my darling Son, Jesus Christ. His birth, life, death, and resurrection. Selah (Psalm 3:8, KJV).

Heavenly Marriage on Earth

Jesus is the husband who is eternally committed and eternally faithful to His beloved (Jer. 31:32, NIV), even when she has been unfaithful and undeserving in her ways. He stands unshaken, pouring His love, grace, mercy, and forgiveness on His beloved (Hosea 3:1, NIV) because His banner over her is *love*, and His love for her is well-known (Song of Sol. 2:4, NIV). This is an excellent place to remember that the most commonly known verse in the bible says, "For God so loved the world ..." (John 3:16, NIV).

If you've been married for over fifty years, you have experienced the bliss that comes with half a century—where the two become one, finishing each other's sentences, sounding alike, looking like a sister and brother with slight resemblances. You may even have jaw-dropping moments of having the same thoughts, and even the same dream in your sleep hours. The blessedness of an equally yoked marriage may occur before the fifty-year point. If you've been married under fifty years, you have yet to experience it.

Congratulations on the number of years you have been married. If you lived to see a hundred years of marriage to the same person, it can *never* be compared to God's marriage to us. It is unlike any marriage here on earth. None can match or top the height, width, depth, intensity, strength, and inseparable love of God (Rom. 8:38–39, NIV).

One may declare and decree that one has found the perfect equally yoked partner in marriage and ministry. For the first five to ten years in the marriage, this may appear to be true. However, going public without the wedding ring and taking photographs without it, generally suggest ruckus inside the relationship. Perhaps one is saying to the other, *I'm willing to leave you in this marriage and become available for someone else.*

Going out in public without a wedding ring is generally done as an ultimatum or a scare tactic, either to get the spouse to change destructive behaviors or to strike the fear of losing the marriage altogether. Certain religions today do not advocate the wearing of jewelry, much less wedding rings.

Nevertheless, at our very best, we still misrepresent the Jesus model of love and marriage. Whether married, single, divorced, or widowed, we are inadequate, are made a little lower than angels, and can never ever be comparable to God.

The Lord is forever unmatchable and unbeatable. Keeping this perspective in mind serves as a spiritual safeguard to cushion the blow of daily disappointments in personal relationships and social networking. Yes, disappointments will come as a part of life, but they can't linger permanently, as long as "Jesus is the *best*" remains your mindset.

Any place in scripture where God's children and prosperous nations rebelled against Him, He is seen as the "committed lover," lavishing forgiveness, compassion, and second chances on an unfaithful, undeserving people. Wherever idolatry occurs, He responds with jealousy to protect and secure His people for His ultimate pleasure and purpose.

Any place on Earth where disloyalty and disappointment occur, rejection, estrangement, separation, and even divorce are the consequences. Humankind in its best effort to tolerate and endure marriage is far below God's ability to love and forgive. Even if this great truth is hard to swallow, the love of God transcends all types of human love and is the only heavenly marriage on Earth.

CHAPTER 12

Characteristics of God

Loving and Just

God is loving enough to save victims and just enough to punish perpetrators. The same angry, wrathful God who punishes the acts of sin and the sinners who committed them is the same God who takes aggressive action to reconcile the estranged into a loving relationship with Himself. Who keeps an unfaithful spouse relationship? Absolutely right! No one!

God, the creator, has a special knack for constructing devices to bring estranged folks back to Himself. We would reconcile with each other if we thought there was something left to benefit from. God reconciles us to Himself because He knows there's nothing good left in us, and He desires a total overhaul and fresh makeover for each of us.

The Just Judge

God lets us plead for relief and present our lamentations (complaints) to Him. As our advocate, He ensures a fair trial, even though He knows our hearts are desperately wicked. Our defense attorney defends our cause, knowing the verdict is fixed. He prosecutes and cross-examines us through the conviction of the Holy Ghost.

God focuses His undivided attention to our case, like a carefully picked jury, summoned to consider every piece of evidence/exhibit for the most accurate final verdict. God is judge, jury, prosecutor, defense attorney, and convictor in the court of Life. He makes all things work out for the good of those who love Him and are called according to His purpose (Rom. 8:28, NIV).

God ordered Barak, a mighty man of valor, to lead the army of Israel into war and defeat the enemy Canaanites and their king, Sisera. Since Barack did not act immediately, God caused a holy woman, judge, and prophetess to summon Barack to obey God's orders. At Barak's request for her company, she led Barack and his army straight into war, defeated their enemies, and returned with the victory, declaring that the Lord had given them the victory.

Justice for All

Twenty years of oppression were going to come to a screeching halt because God wanted justice and peace for His people, the Israelites. He was not going to allow one man's fear to keep the entire country under perpetual oppression. Since both Barack and the children of Israel at one point in time disobeyed God and turned away from Him, He could have punished them and allowed life-long oppression at the hands of the enemy. But God's "just" attributes would not let evil reign over His people.

His justice brought freedom from oppression and forty years of peace for all Israelites to enjoy without violence (Judg. 4–5, KJV). Whether we are as alert as the Prophetess Deborah, knowing what God wants and making it happen, or as complacent as Barack, God does not wish evil nor bondage to reign over us.

Jealous Name/Nature

Another attribute of God is jealousy. To be exact, *El-Qanna* in Hebrew, which means *jealous*. God wants us for Himself. He said "My name is jealous. I'm a jealous God." Therefore the people were commanded not to have any other gods before Him. (Exod. 34:14, KJV). Idolatry is the worship of other gods. Images made of gold, silver, and wood by human hands, then mounted and worshiped as gods, are associated with this verse. On a broader spectrum, idolatry includes any person, place, or thing that has taken God the Creator's place in our lives.

Sly Forms of Idolatry

Idols are those images formed by human hands using earthly materials, such as metal, wood, gold, silver, diamonds, etc. They are also the invisible forms that are hidden inside the heart and cannot be seen with the naked eye. Although they cannot be seen, evidence of their existence is displayed in various behaviors.

Proclivities, secret sins, friends, family, controlled substances, materialistic mindset, houses, vehicles, money, recreational activities, cigarettes, alcohol, gambling, sex-texting, social media addictions—the God of all flesh doesn't like this one bit, He declared, "Thou shall have no other gods before me." He is vexed with a holy vexation with those who worship and bow down to handmade idols, plus the ones that are erected in their hearts. These things steal our time and attention from a daily committed relationship with God (El-Qanna) and provoke Him into aggressive responses.

Holy Jealousy

Jealousy drives Him to pounce, growl, fight, and claw away all threats to His children. As a lioness pounces on the danger drawing near to her cubs and saves them from being a grab-and-go lunch for famished beasts, so are God's protective instincts and jealous attributes. He desires to save us—from our own destructive ways, life-threatening foes, and eternal damnation—and reserve us for Himself, His Glory, and His very own possession, a royal priesthood, a chosen nation to proclaim His excellence (1 Pet. 2:9, NSBV).

To top it all off, like a scoop of vanilla ice cream on top of a slice of hot apple pie, He does not want any of us to perish (Matt. 18:14, NIV)—no, not one. God's just attributes cause Him to scout after us in tireless chases and hot pursuits.

CHAPTER 13

Accounting for Sin

God visits the iniquity of the fathers to the third and fourth generations. Pick any given family, regardless of class or status, and we will find more than just physical resemblances among relatives. There are traceable medical problems, behavior patterns, fetishes, biases, and even similar likes and dislikes going sixty generations back. Despite genetic similarities, each person now has to give an account of himself to God. The father eating sour grapes will no longer set the child's teeth on edge (Jer. 31:29, NIV).

Neither should we continue in the old adage "like father, like son," or "like mother, like daughter." If the father stops sinning but the son continues, the son will be judged for his offenses. If the son stopped his wickedness but the father continues with them, the father will be judged for his own sins (Jer. 31:30, NIV). The days of blaming parents and environmental factors for sin are over. Each person will give an account for their ways to God (Rom. 14:12, NIV).

These things are written so that we might know that we have eternal life—salvation (1 John 5:13 NIV). The price for all sin (offensive words, thoughts, and deeds) is death, but the gift of God is still eternal life (Rom. 6:23 NIV). If we confess our sins to one another and pray for one another, we shall be healed.

We can confess our sins to ourselves by first admitting and owning our faults. We can also reveal our sins one to another as we are invited to pray for each other and receive healing from God. Ultimately, if we confess our sins to God, He is faithful and just to forgive and cleanse us from all unrighteousness.

The price is death. Still, the gift of God is eternal life with an eternal purpose. God's love for you is inseparable and immeasurable (Rom. 8:38–39 NIV). No matter how vile or evil our offenses are, His grace outweighs them all. Accept everything scripture says about God, from the front to the back. It is the inherent, unadulterated word of God. This act of faith puts us right back into the palms of His hands. Once we are in His hands, no human powers can pluck us out. No evil, tremendous or small, can divide His love from us.

CHAPTER 14

Consequences of Sin

*W*hether you describe your sins as hereditary, self-willed, environmental, or all of the above, the soul that sins shall surely die. Whether we commit the seven deadly sins, the six things God hates, or eight woes against the Pharisees; or sin in word, thoughts, deeds, omissions, or commissions; or sin for reasons hereditary, environmental, or self-willed, sin is still sin, and the price for *all* sin is death, regardless of the determinants or classifications. If we break one of the Ten Commandments, we're guilty of breaking all ten of them.

You may satisfy your urge to take revenge, but carefully count the cost. The end of such matters is the glaring danger of a criminal record, hospitalization, death, imprisonment, a lifetime of regrets, and worst of all, a possible derailment of one's faith, destiny, and original purpose. It is better to avoid vices and vengeance, because their outcomes are the same equivalency of death and destruction (Gen. 50:20, Ezek. 18:20, Rom. 6:23, Mal. 2:15 NKJV).

God's Mercies

Although they repeatedly molested and raped her, God's mercy kept her alive through all of their brutish manhandling. He also deterred her from mimicking predatorily behaviors and sustained her faith in God. Although she was raped by a priest, she did not turn to a lifestyle of prostitution for a sense of belonging, nor to substance abuse to anesthetize her pain and traumas. Every outcome is accredited to God and her faith and trust in Him—no magic wands or secrets of her own, just God's pure grace and mercy.

Victims

Typically, victims of childhood abuse and molestation grow up to be predatorial in many different ways. They don't realize it is abnormal behavior until someone skillfully points it out as such.

For some adults, self-sabotaging behaviors come naturally, like breathing air, and feel natural because it was their reality from the cradle. We show mindfulness and sensitivity when we refrain from judging and criticizing others whose normal lifestyle deviates from our standards.

When they were done satisfying the burning lust of their flesh, they left her bleeding, hurting, and crying, with feelings of guilt, shame, and fear. On top of these stuffed emotions, she had a military career, a marriage, children, a high level of education, and an everyday social life, including church membership and a chaplain career.

Oh wow! What appears to be a successful progressive life was a hot mess being consistently saved by God's hands. It was one trial after another, followed by one victory after another. Sometimes it was an uphill battle, with no view of how it would end.

Time-Released Curse

When a seed is planted in the soil, after a while it, sprouts up. The sprout grows into a tree, and the tree bears a specific fruit in its season. Pawpaw trees take five to seven years to grow from a seed buried in the ground. But, just as sure as pawpaw seeds take sprout after many years, so does sexual immorality, even if it comes decades and generations later.

When adults commit the offense of adultery, fornication, or other types of immorality, they're actually planting seeds of corruption. These seeds are bound to sprout up over a period of time, revisiting the child's marriage then ripping it to shreds. A very common example is a spouse (husband or wife) who rekindles an old relationship through social media, leading to an extramarital affair that causes the existing marriage or marriages to end in divorce. Generally, the breakup resembles the pattern of how other relationships ended generations ago.

A strong determination to uproot oneself from old generational patterns, seek personal growth and development, and break the cycle of hereditary offenses is commendable. However, if you are the only one in the marriage with this determination, the door of your marriage is left ajar for old friends, old acquaintances, and old generational curses to return full swing and wreak havoc.

This is one of the reasons the Bible makes it an absolute mandate to be equally yoked. For example, 2 Corinthians 6:14 NKJ teaches us to be not unequally yoked with unbelievers.

When a believing Christian marries a nonbeliever, righteousness and lawlessness are attempting to be one.

In the case of generational curses, it is a challenge being yoked with someone who does not carry the same conviction to break away from hereditary cycles of sin. A chain can only be as strong as its weakest link, and in this instance, the weaker link can be either the husband or the wife. However, if the husband and wife join in with the spirit of God, they present a united front that no devil in hell or generational curse can penetrate.

Before kindling a new relationship for marriage, consider doing the following:

- Power-wash all historical artifacts, pictures, contacts, caches, and old phone numbers. You may even want to buy a brand-new cell phone with a brand-new phone number. The generational curse of sexual immorality only needs one crack, one spark, from one old acquaintance. Then the home wreckage begins.

- Men: Say goodbye to all female best friends from childhood, high school, workplace, church, social media, etc. Every Bride wants to know you have forsaken all others just for her. The less women you have in your profile the greater your chances of a long lasting marriage. Maintain relationship boundaries between immediate family members and the first, second, and distant cousins. You might not be aware of it, but distant relatives are notorious for crossing boundaries and illicit behavioral issues.

- Women: Say goodbye to all male best friends from childhood, high school, workplace, church, social media, etc. you may not plan to trouble your own marriage by cheating with old friends, but old sparks can rekindle under good intentions. Every Groom is comforted to know competitive threats in male factors are disarmed. Maintain relationship boundaries between immediate family members and the first, second, and distant cousins. You might not be aware of it, but distant relatives are notorious crossing boundaries and illicit behavioral issues.

- Pinpoint addictive behaviors and patterns inherited across the family lineage. Seek personal, physical, spiritual, and psychological rehabilitation from illicit sex, drug/alcohol addictions, overspending, overeating, medical problems, criminal activities, trouble with the law, imprisonment, and lack of education, to name a few. These things are to be regarded as potential parasites that eat away at the core of the well-intended relationship if not tackled and dispelled before marriage.

CHAPTER 15

Credit to the Holy Ghost

*T*he Holy Ghost of God is the answer to all the problems in the world today—*problems* meaning being sexually traumatized, heartbroken, sin-bound, taken hostage, sick, diseased, lost, poor, deaf, blind, or impoverished, with nothing intact nor together. *Holiness* means the Holy Ghost. He is the third person of the Godhead, fully complete, lacking nothing. He lacks nothing because He and the Father and the Son are one. The Holy Ghost is God, and God is *holy.*

To be holy, therefore, is to resume the image and likeness of the three in one. From the beginning, this was their intent: "Let us make man in our own image in likeness." Unfortunately, the infiltration of sin marred our desire for the true holiness of God. To escape from the brokenness of today's world is to return to our whole original state—fully complete, whole, lacking nothing, and in a never-ending, close-knit relationship with God. The Spirit Himself draws us back into a relationship with God and the church (John 6:44, Acts 2:47, NIV).

We must be born again (John 3:7 NIV), remade in the image and likeness of our Heavenly Father, Son, and Holy Spirit. We who are being saved must submit ourselves to the ongoing lifelong process of consecration and sanctification by the Office of the Holy Spirit. *Holy* is a prefix in His name. *Spirit* is the process through which everything is accomplished. Not by human might, nor by human power, only by His Spirit (Zech. 4:6, NIV). Under this ministry of the Holy Spirit, the illegal laws of sin working within the human heart (Rom. 7:23, Matt. 15:18, NIV) get arrested, bound, and dispelled from controlling believers' lives. Angels rejoice at this hostile overthrow of the powers of darkness. A new decree and declaration are made because the believer's life is under construction and under the new management of the Holy Ghost.

When God allowed the inauguration of the Holy Ghost in the upper room on the day of Pentecost, it was not just a thing of the past. We must anticipate with great expectation that greater glory is coming, and rain will drench our dwelling places. The joy and merriment of the latter house will excel above the joy and merriment of the former house of God. This will not come with a Jew or gentile restriction; it is for every man under the sun. All nations crave the power of God, whether they realize it or not. All cultures' creeds that cover the face of the earth desire this one great thing: the manifestations of the glory of God Himself (Hag. 2:7, NIV).

In this twenty-first century, millions have surrendered their lives to Jesus Christ and are waiting for spiritual power to testify for Him, work greater works, and resume behaviors exemplary of holiness. This supernatural power from Heaven also made a personal and permanent appearance in my life, empowering me with gifts and graces to do great works preordained by God.

CHAPTER 16

Seek the Baptism

T hanks to the indwelling power of the Holy Spirit. Through Him, I was able to overcome my childhood traumas. Generational habits and vices were uprooted and dispelled from my life. Marriage betrayal, jealousy from in-laws, heartbreaks, unemployment, homelessness, and medical problems, just to mention a few, were made subject to the dynamic working power of the Holy Ghost in my life. Not every trial was stopped. But I was made to bow to the majestic power and anointing God placed in my life. I have suffered many trials and tribulations but overcame them as I submitted to the holy power of the Holy Ghost of God. Praise be to El Shaddai the Almighty one.

Everyone is invited to seek the baptism of the Holy Spirit by first embracing the word of truth, which is the gospel of the grace of God. We have heard and trusted the Word of

Truth; then, after believing, we were sealed with that Holy Spirit of promise (Eph. 1:13, Col. 1:5, KJ21).

Hands-Off

The baptism of the Holy Ghost through the laying on of hands and blowing of breath are possible. The Bible accounts for many receiving spiritual gifts by the laying on of hands. However, no preacher laid hands on me, whispered in my ears, blew in my face, or encamped a circle around me when I received the Holy Ghost in 1993.

To God be all the glory for the supernatural presence of the Holy Ghost who made a grand public entrance into my life over twenty-eight years ago. Today, He is still at work in my dreams, visions, family, home, school, ministry, body, and children.

I was so lost, only God could find me. I was so parched and thirsty, only God could quench and fill me. God could have sent a person or an angel to touch me, but He did it Himself. He used His own hands. He opened His floodgates and showered down on me. He wanted to publicly glorify Himself through me, and that is precisely what He did.

Everyone present, including pastors, preachers, ushers, deacons, mothers, and a packed church, witnessed me enveloped in the Spirit. A swift bopping of my head, a speedy dancing in my feet, an unknown language on my tongue, and a jubilant body movement—it was the moment I heard and believed the Word of Truth, and that's when the Holy Ghost descended upon me in a big crowd of witnesses at midday service.

"She Caught the Holy Ghost"

I heard the mothers of the church, with other onlookers, say, "She caught the Holy Ghost!" Much like a broken record, it was going around the church. Even weeks later, they said, "She caught the Holy Ghost!" Yes, God's Holy Spirit enveloped me while all eyes were on me.

That day, when I came through, I was unable to stand—overwhelmed in the Spirit. The supernatural hand of God reached down from Heaven and sealed me with the Holy Spirit. Oh, what a foretaste of divine glory. Today, I declare and decree all rights reserved for God, and I release total credits to God my Creator. Jesus is my Lord and Savior, sanctifier, consecrator, and baptizer of fire from Heaven.

Go and wait and tarry in Jerusalem until the Spirit of Truth comes. He will bring back to remembrance all truth spoken by God, He will ultimately empower you to do the work God has ordained for you. Emphasis is placed on *He*, the Holy Spirit, because He is our source of energy, motivation, and inspiration to accomplish whatever the Lord would have us do.

The work of the great commission (spreading the gospel to all nations) cannot get accomplished by mere human might nor by human power but, by His Holy Spirit (a supernatural power from heaven). God is the creator of marriage and family relationships but don't get it twisted. A ring on the finger, and a warm body in the bed does not necessarily empower good works. Neither does being single and disengaged.

Being married can limit the quality and quantity of time given to work, because married couple's attention is divided between internal and external matters. In contrast, the unmarried can render more time in good works because their attention is not shared nor divided with a spouse who has priority over others. The unmarried also has more time at hand to avail themselves for good works. Nevertheless, whether married or unmarried each believer must be filled with the Holy

Spirit in order to be an effective witness of the finished works of Jesus Christ and to be an active servant for the Kingdom of God.

Works Of His Spirit

Never limit the works of the Holy Spirit of God to just one specific gender, or a marital status. God used a five-time divorced woman in Samaria to draw the city of men who became believers in Jesus Christ (John 4:18, 29, 30, 39, 41,42 KJV). Bear in mind, there were no digital technology, cell phones nor satellites which allows news to travel far. Therefore, proper credence must be given to the supernatural presence of the Holy Spirit working through the woman and enabling the men of Samaria to come out and see the Messiah for themselves.

God used a married couple name Priscilla and Aquila to strengthen the early Christian church, team up with the Apostle Paul as they lived, worked, and traveled with him. This married couple were also Credited for instructing a major evangelist, Apollos, in the way of God more accurately (Romans 16;3, Acts 18:26 KJV).

Because God is fully sovereign in all matters; He

opened a donkey's mouth and it spoke to Balaam saying, *what have I done to make you beat me three times?* (Numbers 22:21-39 NIV). In another account, God reversed the order of nature and caused a human being Nebuchadnezzar to eat grass like oxen, grow hair like eagles' feathers and nails like birds talons. If we human beings refuse to praise God; He will cause the rocks to cry out hallelujahs. We must now change our minds and admit God can use the married, unmarried, tangible and intangible to further his works by the empowering presence of his Holy Spirit.

CHAPTER 17

A Force to Reckon With

H oliness is what God gives to a victim—divine opportunities to be restored to a safe place, sexual purity, and good works. He may have allowed her to be conceived, raised, affected, and wounded by the hand of the devil called sexual immorality. But He gave that little girl victory. In every incident of molestation and abuse, He showed up and rescued her. More than half a century later, Jesus is still her hero, the bishop of her soul and the captain of her salvation.

Today, He is still her superhero who intercepts, delivers, and sets her free from entrapments, threats, or entanglements. Today, she is a multi-gifted servant, with a five-fold mantel of services. She has a history, résumé, and profile loaded with service in various dimensions, specifically large organizations such as the military, public schools, prisons, and churches. She operates as needed.

Although she was once battered and bruised like a piñata, today she's strong, virtuous, full of great substance and high value, especially to her immediate family, impoverished communities, and those who are of the household of faith:

- **As an apostle**, she refurbished an old prison building for 1,500 convicted felons to come and find hope in faith-based programs and services.

- **As a prophetess**, she hears a word from the Lord in visions and dreams, then imparts the word to those to whom it applies. One morning, she was preparing to go to work when something told her to stay home and call it a day. And so she did. The next day, she returned to work and was briefed with two reports on altercations between inmates and officers inside the chapel while she was away. She is a seer of things that are not yet apparent to others. Her gift hinges on divine-preservation, protection, and the greater good of others.

- **As a pastor of prisoners**, she tended to the re-entry needs of inmates at Florida state's largest female prison of 2,500 convicted felons.

- **As an evangelist**, she preached fiery messages to inmates as they get off the bus, like a military drill sergeant, boisterously projecting the word of God: "Repent, turn away from a life of crime; rehabilitate; return to society a better citizen. Your sons and daughters need a father. Your sons and daughters need you to get your act together." Her cadence was known and respected by staff and inmates alike, and to new convicts just arriving at a reception center where a population of 3,500 transients lived for a temporary period of one year. The revolving door and a captive audience were a dream come true for the evangelist in her.

- **As a teacher**, she served the public school system, specifically in exceptional education. She mainstreamed students with difficulties learning back to general education classes. These students had specific learning disabilities, emotional handicaps, mental handicaps, and ADHD (attention deficit disorder), or sometimes two or three simultaneously.

- **As an advocate**, she takes various assignments and empowerment from the Holy Ghost to serve the least of God's people. Prisoners, the poor, and the needy are among those she feeds, clothes, and shelters. She spearheaded Grace Chapel Ministries in North Las Vegas, with "Doing Good!" as her slogan, from Galatians 6:10 KJV.

It is no wonder the devil tried to kill her as a baby just

three days old, with an omphalitis infection of the umbilical cord. Amazing how the devil's plan failed and was made void and null. The devil must have known the weight of glory God had in store for the little girl. He might have gotten a sneak preview of her preaching the gospel to the poor and prisoners.

The little girl would grow up to be a force to be reckoned with by defying all evil odds set out to destroy her. She became a threat to the kingdom of darkness. She became a noted excellent Christian author, a provider of restorative resources to the poor and needy, and founder of Grace Chapel Ministries in Las Vegas. For such was that heavy anointing invested in her by the Father in Heaven. She now reaches the world through her previously recorded sermons now transcribed into books. She will continue to draw many lost souls in prison and in poverty back to the light of Jesus Christ.

Oh yeah! That naïve, bashful little girl grew up to be a force to reckon with and a threat to the kingdom of darkness. No wonder the devil tried so hard to take her out. God, her Father, knew the plans He had for her life, and no devil in hell or on Earth could thwart them.

If doing good to all people is the outcome of one who

was born in the sin of sexual immorality, something good can happen to every reader of this book. God intended for you to get this book in your hands to remind you of His plans of hope and a future for you.

Regardless of the source of sin—inherited genetics, childhood environment, or individual self-willed—this writer suffered the consequences and overcame them all. Only by God's grace, powerful Holy Spirit, and preset purpose for her particular life did she survive. There was no human formula of her own. The sum total of her good works were like filthy rags, polluted with germs and bacteria (Isa. 64:6, NIV). Only the loving-kindness and tender mercies of God saved her.

Holy is the God-fearing woman she became. She serves many with similar backgrounds and scars. Holy also is the God whose hands reached down from Heaven and rescued her repeatedly. Holy are His fingers that pen the books of her life, on every page of which His fingerprints are visible.

Takeaways

Victims do not have to become predators. Just because you were hurt once upon a time by some church, clergy, stranger, or relative doesn't mean you should grow up to be just like them (abusers). You do not have a license to judge and condemn others straight to hell. You may be the earthly owner of houses land and cars but you do not have ownership nor monopoly of a heaven nor hell. Stop it! The curse of inflicting unnecessary pain must be broken. The curse of blaming others for how you are must also be broken. You are responsible for your own behaviors. No one in your past can account to God for you. Judge and evaluate yourself. Or you could get a dose of your own medicine. (Mark 7:1 KJV). Be wise, and choose blessings over curses.

CHAPTER 18

Unholy Acts

*W*icked were the men and their heinous crimes against a little girl. The Holy Bible says the wicked are like worthless chaff, scattered by the wind. They will be condemned at the time of judgment. Sinners will have no place around the godly (Ps. 1:4–5, NIV). These were the sinful acts perpetrated against her:

- **Fondled by her uncle at Saturday midday matinees**, where he seated her conveniently near the booth where he sold tickets. After sales, he tippy-toed his way in the dark to where she sat and began his nasty finger strokes, plucks, pats, and tugs until she began to burn, bleed, and squirm her body from side to side. His fingers felt like hard stone bruising her tender parts. There was no escape from his firm grip pinning her to the seat, forcing her to remain steady. Tears like fire streamed down her cheeks. *"Shh! Shh! Shh!"* he said. "Don't be so loud!" But quiet squeals, whimpers, cries, and snot still came out of her. In the end, he whipped out a large piece of cherry-flavored candy to pacify her— that is, until the next Saturday matinee.

- **Buggered by a priest every day after school** in second grade. She would make her way helter-skelter up the winding staircase in the back of the church's presbytery where Father Vincent lived. Pounds of leftover communion bread (wafers) were stashed in brown burlap bags, and there was always a brown paper bag full just for the little girl. Poured in a bowl with sugar and milk, she ate them as her favorite after-school snack.

An old white-haired scruffy man with a fat tummy welcomed her with open arms. Her face squished against his belly in a bear hug. She remembered his heavy rapid breathing and the coffee stench on his breath. He laid her face down on his twin cot-bed, removed her undies, then, after satisfying himself with her innocence, slumped his husky bear body on top of her frail tiny child's body to catch his breath, shallow, short, and gasping. He remained still. Then something wet and slimy with an awful smell jetted out of him. *Yuck! What is that nasty smell?* the little girl thought to herself. She could have suffocated under his heavy body weight collapsed on her.

Another bag of wafers was reserved for the girl for tomorrow's after-school snack. His bribes of communion wafers for anal buggery continued until the little girl moved out of Georgetown with her family.

- **Indecent exposure of a child pedophile** across the street grabbed her attention from her childhood playground. He recklessly agitated his genitals to an oblivious state, all as he stared, his eyes fixed on the little girl. This must've been traumatizing for her, because she has no recollection of what happened next—whether she was shocked, frozen, screamed, or took off running for help. She has completely forgotten the after details but remembers the indecent exposure.

- **Slapped across the kitchen floors** by the big hand of a strong, tall, muscular uncle. The little girl was stealing sugar from the sugar jar in the kitchen. The hit flung her tiny body across the wooden kitchen floor. The slap across her small face numbed the entire left side, ear, cheek, and jaws.

  Later in her adult life, she had a dream about a brown snake that slithered into her ear canal. She could not pull it out, no matter how hard she tried. About a month after the dream, she suffered sudden episodes of vertigo. They said it was due to dislodged crystals in the inner eardrums. After a while, the structural damage within the ear canal was discovered.

- **Suffered infidelity**—In one account, she poured her heart and soul into him. She prayed for divine protection and God's presence over him as he lay to sleep and slumber in his bed. *Sweet dreams!* As her prayers dispatched angels, God's presence, and His richest blessings over him. She made sure she did everything she thought a woman should do: cook, clean, nurture my children, support his business ideas, validate his feelings, listen to his concerns, wash and fold his laundry, clip his toenails, be a perfect caregiver during the day and a sexy bunny during the night.

On another account, she poured her heart and soul out the exact same way, adding expensive gifts, frequent house parties, monthly romantic surprises, and date-night outings at elaborate places. The reciprocation was little to none, and the little he did show was far less than what he received from her.

Each breakup struck her heart like a dozen bumblebee stings. Venomous were the stings, and excruciating were the extractions of them. Well, as if birthing an elephant, she hunched over, growled out the pain, gnashed her teeth, and suffered through to the end. Question: Which is worse? The wooing of the heart for a few decades, then crushing it to pieces? Or an abrupt and unannounced stabbing and plummeting it to pieces?

Survivors of childhood traumas and repeated betrayal, such as those the author suffered, take time to shake off. The time frame for recovery varies from person to person. Some will take ten years, some fifty, and others a lifetime. While history proves God can save, heal, and deliver at a moment's notice, He does not always move in a hurry. Nevertheless, sufferers must neither imitate the ways of predators nor seek revenge for the pain and suffering inflicted. It is the expected norm to sulk, grieve, and lament over the struggles and trials in one's past.

A victim turned predator with revenge is just a knee-jerk reaction and work of the flesh in retaliation. There are other ways of settling a score than taking revenge. Rest assured that adulterers, molesters, pedophiles, rapists, and wrongdoers will give an account to God for themselves someday (Rom. 14:12, KJ21). So there you go! God settles the scores. The scores are too big in number, too wide in offenses for us to handle. Our shoulders are not made wide and strong enough to carry our own burdens. But God is the ultimate avenger and record-keeper who knows how to tally up the scores, bring everyone into account, and close out the books. So we must trust the master tabulator to settle the scores.

The following is the author's advice to every reader of *Fifty Shades of Red*:

1. Deepen and extend your trust and faith in God during and after your traumas.

2. If you don't have a relationship with Jesus Christ, begin reading the book of John. You will discover your faith and a desire to develop it.

3. Answer His call to holiness. Reserve yourself for His uses and follow His commandments.

4. Stay ready for the rapture by keeping your eyes on the clouds for His return.

5. Get caught in compliance with His principles.

6. Get intimate with God. A close-knit relationship with God helps to prepare a survivor for serving other injured parties in similar situations.

7. Revenge, retaliation, and a deep desire to avenge are contrary to the behaviors of holiness. So follow these tips given in *Fifty Shades of Red*.

8. Send the author a letter on how this book benefited you.

Start distribution of those 490 forgiveness cards Jesus referenced when Peter asked about forgiving his brothers: not seven times seven, but seventy times seven, Jesus replied (Matthew 18:22 KJV). Don't decide it is impossible to do, because the writer of this book you are reading was in fact cornered, crushed, and stampeded with many afflictions and did not have anything left inside of her to distribute to anyone.

CHAPTER 19

To Hell and Back

She feared what would become of her soul if she did not forgive her offenders. The fear of God, fiery pits of hell, and an openly real out-of-body experience in which she was trapped in hell with no way out except by the name of Jesus brought her to ask, "Which is the way out of here?" Someone pointed to the left and said, "Over there!" But a red blazing fire covered that exit.

In a frantic tailspin to find a safe exit, she found that there was none. Every direction was kindling a reddish blaze of fire. There were several depths and tiers of darkness. Dead bodies had been laid side by side in rank pillage and black clothes, identified as those who forsook their habitat. The foulest stench filled the dead atmosphere.

She opened her eyes and discovered she was still in her bed and in a beautiful home, with no fire or darkness around her. Lying still in her bed with both hands lifted up, she inhaled and exhaled awesomely clean air, with no more smoky corpse fumes. With deep appreciation, she praised God that He did not leave her down there in those stinky smelly pits of hell. In her out-of-body experience, she had screamed the name Jesus and was propelled up back to earth. God spared her life from the burning lake of fire.

Regardless of past guilt, shame, and pain, we cannot afford to engage in vigilante actions. Grace Chapel, having experienced the horrors of hell, came back with the urgency to forgive everyone indebted to her—past, present, and future. She commands her soul on a daily basis to live, forgive, and love exactly the way God wants her to: a *new* way in Jesus. That's the name she heard herself calling when the spirit of God ushered her back to her body inside her bedroom. More details of her out-of-body experience will be featured in her next book, *700 Paths To Hell*.

Complimenting and imitating the ways and thoughts of the Highest and Most Holy God—what does it all mean? The mere fact that we are alive today could mean that God gave us a story about himself to write and a message for the rest of the world. We must now witness to others how God saves, heals, and delivers.

Holiness is quite an action word—lived-out behaviors that are in compliance with God's word. It has nothing to do with long dresses, coverings on the head, or the absence of cosmetics. Decency, order, and moderation are expedient to holiness and include:

- evaluating the heart daily
- considering which areas must be changed
- permitting the Holy Spirit to pray on your behalf
- using the gifts of tongues to pray in the spirit
- fasting over matters too stubborn to move
- breaking away from generational curses
- living life in peace and harmony with God and people

Remembering such is expedient to holiness, and without it, no one gets to see God.

A Few of the Author's Nighttime Pieties

- Go to bed with soft melodious instrumental gospel songs, psalms, praise, and worship music.

- Anoint your head with oil before you sleep, and any aching part of your body.

- Sleep with a notebook and pencil beside your pillow and record your dreams and visions. You will find God's guidance, warnings, and promises for your life.

- Take time within the course of your day and week to reflect on your dream journal.

- Pay strict attention to everything God reveals and promises; it will come to pass.

CHAPTER 20

Fifty Shades of Red

*T*hese are fifty different shades of red:

1. scarlet

2. vermillion

3. crimson

4. ruby

5. chili pepper

6. cardinal

7. auburn

8. burgundy

9. carmine

10. rosewood

11. fleurette

12. shiraz

13. raspberry wine

14. dark cherry

15. candy apple

16. maroon

17. hibiscus

18. turkey red

19. Japanese

20. strawberry

21. dark rose

22. light rose

23. blood

24. currant

25. wine

26. fire engine

27. cranberry

28. octane

29. bright orange

30. tart

31. barn

32. magenta

33. Indian

34. salmon

35. tuscan

36. watermelon

37. Spanish bread

38. rusty

39. chocolate cosmos

40. plum

41. rose vale

42. cadmium

43. coral

44. garnet

45. persimmon

46. poppy

47. russet

48. cerise

49. fuchsia

50. henna

Regardless of shade or hue, each one still belongs to the family of the color red.

Similarly, there are at least seven hundred different sins in the world, and these are depicted in my next book, entitled *700 Paths To Hell*. The price for *all* sin is still death, regardless of the determinants or classification. If we are guilty of any one of the 700 offenses, we are actually guilty of all. We must be able to see our hopelessness and need for salvation.

There are two main shades of red used in scripture: crimson and scarlet. *Elliott's Commentary for English Readers* explains that these were the colors of the robes worn by the princes Isaiah preached to. The sins committed by God's people in their past were deep and dark, ingrained as the stain of blood. Regardless of the deepened stains of sin, God was willing to make them white as snow and white as wool, under one condition: that they would come and reason together with him.

They would have an open forum to state their case against God, and God would in turn state His case against them. Not that man and God are ever on the same equal plane, but God is so compassionate, with all power to judge and destroy in the blink of an eye, that He was willing to sit and talk with them. His invitation was of such a friendly nature that it would disarm and remove fears and apprehensions that would get in the way of a continued ongoing holy relationship with God. Jehovah God promised that, no matter how deeply and darkly stained within we may be, He delights Himself in discharging all and leave us with a restored purity.

The people of God did very well at blackening their souls, and God was willing to wash them of all their guilty sins and stains just to bring them back together where they belong in fellowship with Him. Men may dye their souls to this or that hue, but to bleach them was the work of God. He alone can transform them so that they should be white as snow (Mark 9:3 ESV). After He makes our souls spotless and pure, He looks on us with the same favor as if we had never committed a single offense.

In the days of the prophet Isaiah, God's people Israel blackened their souls with the hues of rebellion, idolatry, injustice, and corruption. Together, they were categorized as crimson and scarlet. Categories of shades and color schemes are used to symbolize the deepness and darkness of the stains sin leaves behind in the human soul. However, some of us are black as soot.

In the twenty-first century times we are living in, the Church has blackened itself with sins of unrighteousness, lack of holiness, and at least fifty more she often ignores or fails to address. Just as in the days of the prophet Isaiah, God is extending a universal invitation to return into fellowship with Him, to rekindle the relationship we had with Him before we were born. As a result, we become the epitome of purity, as He desires us to be holy. His is the divine scrub that removes every ingrained stain of sin. Therefore, He lifts His voice and calls out in admonition to us: "Come now, and let us reason together ... though your sins are like scarlet, they shall be as white as snow; though they are red like crimson, they shall be as wool." (Isaiah 1:18, NKJV).

The end result of obeying the Lord's admonition would be a purging, spiritual circumcision of the heart, restoration of a sacred relationship with God and man, and full restoration of purity and holiness to the Church. The method to His madness is pretty simple: The Lord is returning for a Church that is without spot or wrinkle. Therefore, He is persistently and feverishly preparing and fitting us for the skies—that is, those of us who want to go to Heaven.

The following are fifty types of sins with fill-in the blank lessons to remember. The first thirteen are pre-answered and the remaining forty two are for you to test your own intelligence quotient. Write out your previous knowledge of each sin, then investigate what the Bible has to say about it. Fill in the blank lines with your explanations and individual applications. This exercise will sharpen your awareness of sin, and increase your thirst for righteousness.

1. **Being a man with a Reuben spirit of uncontrolled lust** (Gen. 35:22, Gen. 49:1, KJ21): This kind of man would take any person's place just to get his sense of pleasure. If his significant other is not available, he will turn to his father's woman, his own sister, daughter, mother, niece, neighbor's child, and if none of these, then he will turn to animals and

manufactured Manichaeans. His character trait is cowardliness. He scopes out the opportune time to strike, then operates in privacy with his victims to avoid getting caught by others.

2. **Being a man with a Laban spirit of trickery** (Gen. 29:18-30, KJ21). This man will trick the living daylights out of his victim. He will arrange stipulations, sign contracts, and include witnesses to his promise. His character trait is business-minded, yet dishonesty, filled with deception and manipulation, rules his heart. More than likely, these kinds of trickery run in the bloodline, and he's living in a generational curse. He can be regarded as a relative to the father of all lies, but to decipher them apart.

3. **Being a man with Amnon raping relative spirit** (2 Sam. 13, KJ21). This man is unable to maintain genetic relations and boundaries. He crosses any and all barriers just to get with his victim. He has performing-arts skills that lures his victims into his bed. A skilled actor who can shake sickness very well, he's full of hidden agendas and will never

say the truth about what he really wants. He plays on the innocence and naivety of his victims. As his concocted scenario unfolds, his real personality comes to light. He is bipolar in the sense that he's totally loving or totally hateful toward his victim, the latter especially when the climax is over. He will either kill the victim or give the victim over to be killed. Multiple personalities can never be trusted.

4. **Being a man with unnatural affections for another man—homosexuality** (Rom. 1:27, KJ21). This man starts out with identity confusion. *Who am I? Where did I come from? How am I supposed to behave? Who am I supposed to be?* His main goal is to be romantically attractive and sexually involved with the same sex or gender. He displays a consistent pattern of sexual orientation, enduring emotional, romantic, and/or sexual attraction to men of the same behaviors. Character traits are seclusion and secrecy to avoid judgmental criticisms from others, but in today's age, behaviors are more open and public than ever before. The rainbow is

a symbol representing their community. The term *pride* is often associated with their lifestyle. Those who are not ready to come out of the closet would get married as a cover-up, but telltale signs of homosexuality will surface during the marriage, such as occasional display of effeminate behaviors, unmanly ways typical of a woman, and the buttocks is an absolute mandate in sex.

5. **Being a woman with natural affections for another woman—lesbianism** (Rom. 1:26, KJ21). *Where did I come from? How am I supposed to behave? Who am I supposed to be?* Her main goal is to be romantically attractive and sexually involved with the same sex or gender. She displays a consistent pattern of sexual orientation, enduring emotional, romantic, and or sexual attraction to women of the same behaviors. Character traits are seclusion and secrecy to avoid judgmental criticisms from others. However, in today's age, behaviors are now more open and public than ever before. The rainbow is a symbol representing their community. The term

pride is often associated with their lifestyles. Those who are not ready to come out of the closet would get married as a cover-up with tell-tale signs that surface during the marriage, such as display of masculine behaviors typical of a man and excessive time out with a possessive girlfriend or a clique.

6. **Being a person who has sex with animals—bestiality** (1 Cor. 15:38–39, Gen. 2:20–22, KJ21). This kind of man has a deterrent within himself that is against the natural relations with a woman's body. Perhaps some were hurt in the past by a female authority of some kind—a mother, grandmother, stepmother. In some cases, a female teacher, sister, aunt, or cousin did something to discourage him from natural relationships with women. Regardless of their past, animals are their only objects of romance, affection, and sexual intercourse. The same can be said about a woman whose personal preference is animals. These people don't get along very well with human beings, so they revert to unnatural animal relationships that cross over from a normal

pet relationship to a simulation of human-to-human relationships (Gen. 1:25–28, Exo. 22:19–20, Deut. 27:21–22, Lev. 20:15–16, Lev.18:22–30, 2 Tim. 3:1–5, Rom. 12:1–2, Rom.1:24–25, 81:12, Eph. 5:11–13, Ps. 7:11, Gal. 5:19–24, Ps. 79:10–11, Jude 1:7, KJ21).

7. **Anyone sleeping with someone else's spouse— adultery** (Matt. 19:18; Gen. 39:7–9; Exod. 20:14, Deut. 22:22; Lev. 20:10-12, Matthew 5:28; 2 Pet. 2:14, KJ21). Their insatiable appetites have no end but are a continuum of greed, discontent, selfishness, and lasciviousness, all accompanying their prodding toward people who are already married. They like to sell themselves as faithful and committed family men or women. That's what they will say with their lips. And for a short period of time, they will prove themselves strongly committed to the relationship. After a while, however, the real motive and fiber of their existence comes to life, and it's usually opposite from what they initially claimed to be. Time is the revealing factor of the true characteristics of an adulterous man or woman. Sometimes five,

ten, fifteen, or even twenty years go by before the real person lying dormant is revealed. Displays of flirtatious behaviors, lengthy hours on social media, lengthy hours on the phone, unaccounted-for whereabouts, extra cellphone and money stashed, frequent mad dashes to the store, and sudden new clothes in the closet are telltale signs that you are in a cheating relationship with an adulterer and it's just a matter of time before it's over.

8. **Being a person who brings harm to a child— pedophile** (Rom. 1:31; 2 Tim. 3:2, Matt. 18: 1–14, 18:6, 18:10, KJ21). According to the DSM-IV, *pedophilia* is defined as a mental disorder that involves a persistent sexual interest in prepubescent children, manifested in thoughts, fantasies, purchases, sexual arousal, or sexual behavior. These people are extremely self-centered and unaware of the emotional trauma and lifelong scars they are inflicting on the victim child. Even if you sat them down to explain, there's a cognitive disconnect that prevents sensitivity of the heart. In America, sex

offenders are required to report their dwellings and change of addresses to the local police department, because no matter where they are relocated, they are likely to repeat their offenses.

9. **Afraid to confess Jesus to people** (John 12:42, KJ21). These people have no understanding of God's power and presence, so they yield themselves to the minuscule presence of people.

10. **Unjustified anger—wrath** (Prov. 27:4, 29:22; Exod. 6:9; 2 Cor. 12:20, KJ21). This is the kind of person who is a sitting volcano waiting to erupt. The eruption and explosion will take place over the smallest slightest thing.

11. **Anger towards your brother** (Matt. 5:22, KJ21). This person has no idea how God feels about his anger issues and how close he is to the dangers of hell when he chooses this emotion.

12. **Anxiety** (Phil. 4:6, KJ21). Where there is a failure to pray, there is worry about uncertain outcomes, and where there is worry about uncertain outcomes, there is the presence of anxiety.

13. **Arguing** (Prov. 17:14, 18:6; Titus 3:9; 2 Tim. 2:23, KJ21). To share one's viewpoint with persuasive evidence may sway others to a certain favorable outcome. But how well does the evidence stand up in God's court of judgment? Remember when arguing that God's view is the only correct one.

For the next thirty-seven shades of sins, write down in the spaces provided your previous knowledge of what the Bible says about it and how you plan to comply and apply.

14. **Arrogance**, swelling pride (Mark 7:22; Isa. 2:17; Rom. 1:30; 2 Cor. 11:20, KJ21)

Previous knowledge _____

_____

_____

What the Bible says _____

_____

_____

My plan to comply _____

_____

_____

15. **Ashamed**, hiding your light for Jesus (Matt. 5:14–16; Luke 9:26; Rom. 10:11, KJ21)

Previous knowledge _____

_____

_____

What the Bible says _____

_____

_____

My plan to comply _____

_____

_____

16. **Ashamed** of Jesus and His words (Mark 8:38 ESV)

Previous knowledge _____

_____

_____

What the Bible says _____

_____

_____

My plan to comply _____

_____

_____

17. **Assault** (Exod.21:18 -19, Acts 14:5 NKJV)

Previous knowledge _____

_____

_____

What the Bible says _____

_____

_____

My plan to comply _____

_____

_____

18. **Astrology** (Deut. 4:19; 17:3–7; Isa. 47:13, 14; Acts 7:42; Ezek. 8:16, KJ21)

Previous knowledge _____

_____

_____

What the Bible says _____

_____

_____

My plan to comply _____

_____

_____

19. **Being scornful** (Ps.1:1, Prov. 9:12, 24:9 TPT)

Previous knowledge _____

_____

_____

What the Bible says _____

_____

_____

My plan to comply _____

_____

_____

20. **Seeking a sign** (Matt. 16:4; Luke 11:29, KJ21)

Previous knowledge _____

_____

_____

What the Bible says _____

_____

_____

My plan to comply _____

_____

_____

21. **Not seeking first the Kingdom of God** (Matt. 6:33, KJ21)

Previous knowledge _____

_____

_____

What the Bible says _____

_____

_____

My plan to comply _____

_____

_____

22. **Selfishness** (Phil. 2:21; 2 Tim 3:2; 3 John 9–11, KJ21)

Previous knowledge _____

_____

_____

What the Bible says _____

_____

_____

My plan to comply _____

_____

_____

23. **Selfish ambition** (Gal. 5:19, 20, NIV)

Previous knowledge _____

_____

_____

What the Bible says _____

_____

_____

My plan to comply _____

_____

_____

24. **Self-righteous, high-minded** (Luke 16:15; Rom. 11:20; Job 9:20; Matt. 5:20, KJ21)

Previous knowledge _____

_____

_____

What the Bible says _____

_____

_____

My plan to comply _____

_____

_____

25. **Self-serving** (Luke 9:23, KJ21)

Previous knowledge _____

_____

_____

What the Bible says _____

_____

_____

My plan to comply _____

_____

_____

26. **Self-willed** (2 Pet. 2:10, KJ21)

Previous knowledge _____

_____

_____

What the Bible says _____

_____

_____

My plan to comply _____

_____

_____

27. **Sex outside marriage—fornication** (1 Cor. 5:11, 6:18, 20; Exod. 22:16, 17, KJ21)

Previous knowledge _____

_____

_____

What the Bible says _____

_____

_____

My plan to comply _____

_____

_____

28. **Not even a hint of sexual immorality** (Eph. 5:3, NIV)

Previous knowledge _____

_____

_____

What the Bible says _____

_____

_____

My plan to comply _____

_____

_____

29. **Sex with a prostitute** (1 Cor. 6:15–18, NIV)

Previous knowledge _____

_____

_____

What the Bible says _____

_____

_____

My plan to comply _____

_____

_____

30. **Sex with a virgin—marry her** (Deut. 22:28, 29, NIV)

Previous knowledge _____

_____

_____

What the Bible says _____

_____

_____

My plan to comply _____

_____

_____

31. **Sex with a virgin (betrothed—if she doesn't cry out, both die)** (Deut. 22:23, 24 NIV)

Previous knowledge _____

_____

_____

What the Bible says _____

_____

_____

My plan to comply _____

_____

_____

32. **Sex with a virgin (betrothed—if she cries out, he dies)** (Deut. 27:20–23, NIV)

Previous knowledge _____

_____

_____

What the Bible says _____

_____

_____

My plan to comply _____

_____

_____

33. **Sex with a relative—cursed** (Deut 27:20-23, NIV)

Previous knowledge _____

_____

_____

What the Bible says _____

_____

_____

My plan to comply _____

_____

_____

34. **Idol (worthless)—shepherd leaving the flock**
(John 10:12; Zech. 11:17, KJ21)

Previous knowledge _____

_____

_____

What the Bible says _____

_____

_____

My plan to comply _____

_____

_____

35. **Shepherd—not searching for God's flock** (Ezek. 34:6-8, NIV)

Previous knowledge _____

_____

_____

What the Bible says _____

_____

_____

My plan to comply _____

_____

_____

36. **Shepherd—not feeding God's flock** (Ezek. 34:8, NIV)

Previous knowledge _____

_____

_____

What the Bible says _____

_____

_____

My plan to comply _____

_____

_____

37. **Shepherd—not strengthen the diseased** (Ezek. 34:4, NIV)

Previous knowledge _____

_____

_____

What the Bible says _____

_____

_____

My plan to comply _____

_____

_____

38. **Shepherd—did not bind up that which was broken** (Ezek. 34:4, NIV)

Previous knowledge _____

_____

What the Bible says _____

_____

_____

My plan to comply _____

_____

_____

39. **Shepherd—did not bring again that which was driven away** (Ezek. 34:4, NIV)

Previous knowledge _____

_____

_____

What the Bible says _____

_____

_____

My plan to comply _____

_____

_____

40. **Shepherd—ruled with cruelty** (Ezek. 34:4, NIV)

Previous knowledge _____

_____

What the Bible says _____

_____

_____

My plan to comply _____

_____

_____

41. **Enticing a nation to sin** (1 Kings 14:16, NIV)

Previous knowledge _____

_____

_____

What the Bible says _____

_____

_____

My plan to comply _____

_____

_____

42. **Know how to do good, but don't do it** (James 4:17 NIV)

Previous knowledge _____

_____

What the Bible says _____

_____

_____

My plan to comply _____

_____

_____

43. **Mocking sin—fools** (Prov. 14:9) and **not ashamed of your sin** (Jer. 8:12, NIV)

Previous knowledge _____

_____

_____

What the Bible says _____

_____

_____

My plan to comply _____

_____

_____

44. **Not confessing your sin** (1 John 1:9; James 5:16; Ps. 32:5; Prov. 28:13, NIV)

Previous knowledge _____

_____

_____

What the Bible says _____

_____

_____

My plan to comply _____

_____

_____

45. **Saying you have not sinned** (1 John 1:10 TPT)

Previous knowledge _____

_____

_____

What the Bible says _____

_____

_____

My plan to comply _____

_____

_____

46. **Refuse to admit you are a sinner** (Jere. 8:6; 1 John

1:8, 10, NIV)

Previous knowledge _____

_____

_____

What the Bible says _____

_____

_____

My plan to comply _____

_____

_____

47. **Refuse to confess your sins** (1 John 1:9, NIV)

Previous knowledge _____

_____

_____

What the Bible says _____

_____

_____

My plan to comply _____

_____

_____

48. **Slander—backbiters** (Mark 7:20-23, Rom. 1:30, 2 Cor. 12:20 TPT)

Previous knowledge _____

_____

_____

What the Bible says _____

_____

_____

My plan to comply _____

_____

_____

49. **Slandering your neighbor in secret** (Ps. 101:5, NIV)

Previous knowledge _____

_____

_____

What the Bible says _____

_____

_____

My plan to comply _____

_____

_____

50. **Smoking** (Rom. 12:1; 13:14; 1 Cor. 3:16–18, 6:20; 2

Cor. 4:10; 1 Pet. 1:15; 1 Thess. 4:4–5, NIV)

Previous knowledge _____

_____

_____

What the Bible says _____

_____

_____

My plan to comply _____

_____

_____

CONCLUSION

*A*ccept God's invitation to come and reason with Him (Isaiah 1:18 TPT). Give God your complaints and grievances. Tell Him why you think you are the way you are. Explain yourself by the hereditary (parental) sins you were born into. Call to account the environmental sins you grew up in, and confess those sins that you know are self-willed—that you have committed because you enjoyed them and you wanted to do them, and you need God to whip it out of you with his pruning hook, plowing sheer, Holy Ghost fire, cleansing hyssop, and fuller's soap (Joel 3:10, Luke 3:16, Psalm 51:7, Malachi 3:2, KJ21)

The Lord's Prayer is the right prayer for everyone who has sinned and fallen short of the glory of God. Jesus said two main things: if we call on the name of Jesus we shall be saved, and that when we pray, we should say:

Our Father Which Art in Heaven Hallowed be thy name. Thy kingdom come, thy will be done, in Earth as it is in heaven. Give us this day our daily bread and forgive us our debts, as we forgive our debtors. And lead us not into temptation but deliver us from Evil for thine is the kingdom, and the power and the glory, forever and ever. Amen! (Matt. 6:9-13, KJV)

I pray that *Fifty Shades of Red* has been a blessing to you. Make notes in the margins on each page that is relevant to you, and keep this book at hand and at your fingertips to reread and listen to as many times and as often as you wish, and to your heart's content. Pass it on to those to whom you think it will be a blessing. Thank you very much for reading *Fifty Shades of Red*.

Printed in the United States
by Baker & Taylor Publisher Services